Quilt Block Party

Series #2 - Baskets and Flowers
© 1989 by Eleanor Burns

Quilt in a Day, Inc.

1955 Diamond Street

San Marcos, CA 92069

Printed in the United States of America

Table of Contents

Yardage 1

Block One Cactus Flower 3

Completing the First Diagonal Row 5

Block Two Basket of Scraps 9

Block Three Flower Basket 11

Block Four English Ivy 13

Block Five Cherry Basket 15

Block Six Patchwork Posy 19

Block Seven Star Basket 23

Block Eight Pine Tree 25

Block Nine Carolina Lily 27

Block Ten Tulip 31

Block Eleven Dobbin's Fan 35

Block Twelve Patch Blossoms 39

Finishing the Quilt 41

Baskets and Flowers Quilt

Make a new block in a different basket or flower design every session and set the twelve blocks together on the point in diagonal rows. Each block can be constructed in one hour or less with easy assembly sewing methods. Nine blocks are made from strips, squares, and rectangles, while three blocks also use template patterns provided.

Approximate Finished Size: 65" x 82"

Twelve 12" Square Finished Blocks

Yardage

Choose the colors for your quilt as you would choose the flowers for your garden; soft pastels or sparkling primaries for your blossoms and greens for your leaves and stems. Your basket fabrics should complement your choices for flowers and leaves. Use this yardage when making the twelve blocks throughout the series.

In addition, mix the scales of your prints. Choose small and medium scale prints, and solids, or ones that look like solids from a distance.

Yardage for the Blocks

Light Background

1 yd. first light

1 yd. second light

Flower Colors

1/2 yd. first medium

1/2 yd. second medium

1/2 yd. first dark

Leaf and Stem Colors

1/2 yd. medium

1/2 yd. dark

Basket Colors

1/2 yd. medium

1/2 yd. dark

Yardage for Side and Corner Triangles, and Solid Squares

Choose a large scale floral print that coordinates with the colors of the baskets and flowers.

If you choose to individually cut out one motif of the floral print and repeat it in all the solid squares, you will need to purchase additional fabric.

2 yds. large scale print Cut the largest pieces first.

Side Triangles:

(3) 18" squares

Cut into fourths on the diagonals.

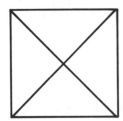

Corner Triangles:

(1) 13 1/2" square

Cut into fourths on the diagonals.

Solid Squares:

(6) 12 1/2" squares

Yardage for Borders and Backing

First Border Purchase additional yardage of one of the light or medium fabrics used in the blocks.

3/4 yd. Cut into (7) 3 1/2" x 45" strips.

Second Border Purchase additional yardage of one of the medium or dark fabrics used in the blocks.

1 1/4 yds. Cut into (7) 5 1/2" x 45" strips.

Backing Purchase additional yardage of a light color.

4 yds. Cut in half. Remove the selvages. Seam together.

Bonded Batting and Optional Binding

Unquilted Blocks with Quick Turn Finish

If you do not wish to machine quilt each individual block, but prefer a "quick turn" finish once all the unquilted blocks are sewn together, do not purchase the batting until the last block is completed. You may select a thick batting that shows dimension when the layers are tied together.

Heavy Bonded Batting

One piece 68" x 85"

Machine Quilted Blocks with Binding Finish

If you wish to machine quilt the individual block following each Quilt Block Party, purchase your lightweight batting at the first Quilt Block Party.

Lightweight Bonded Batting

One piece 68" x 85"

Binding

3/4 yd. same medium or dark fabric as last border

Cut into (8) 3" x 45" strips.

Supplies Needed

Rotary cutter, gridded cutting mat, 6" x 24" ruler with 45° line, (6" x 12" ruler with 45° line optional), 12 1/2" Square Up ruler, 6" square ruler, marking pencil, magnetic seam guide, neutral thread, soft nylon filament invisible thread, scissors, 2 skeins embroidery floss. Machine Quilting Supplies (Optional) binder clips, safety pins

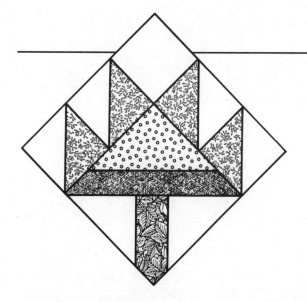

Cactus Flower

Pioneers moving westward used quilts on the trip for warmth and protection, or as packing or, all too often, as burying cloths. Imagine the pioneer women's relief as they spotted the beautiful blanket of desert flowers on the thresh-hold of their final destination, California. Perhaps they recreated that memory by designing this easy pattern for one of the first quilts they made for their new home. Cactus Flower, also known as Texas Flower, first appeared in *Ladies' Art Company* in 1898.

Choose one light background, two flower colors, and two leaf colors.

Cutting Instructions

Layer Cut with Right Sides Together:

(1) 5" x 10" light background color
(1) 5" x 10" first medium flower color

(1) 9" square light background color
(1) 9" square second medium flower color
Cut in half on the diagonal. Eliminate one triangle of each.

(1) 4 1/2" square light background color

(1) 2" x 13" strip first leaf color

(1) 2 1/2" x 6 1/2" strip second leaf color

Use a full and accurate 1/4" seam allowance and 15 stitches per inch.

Sewing the Four

1. With the 5" x 10" pieces right sides together, draw on 5" square lines.

2. Draw on diagonal lines.

3. Sew a 1/4" seam on both sides of the diagonal lines. Press.

4. Cut apart on all lines.

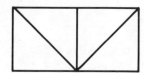

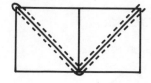

5. Press the seams to the darker side.

6. Arrange in this order with the 4 1/2" light square:

7. Flip the second pieces right sides together to the first pieces.

8. Assembly line sew by butting them behind each other.

9. Add the 4 1/2" pieced square to the second set. Clip the threads. Press.

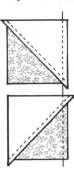

Sewing the

1. On the flower triangle, measure and draw a line 1 1/2" in from the edge on the right side.

2. Line up and center the edge of the 2" x 13" leaf strip with the penciled line, right sides together.

3. Sew 1/4" from the penciled line.

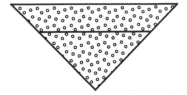

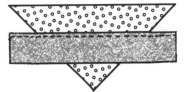

4. Press down and flat.

5. Trim the strip even with the triangle from the wrong side.

6. Press under the long raw edges on the 2 1/2" x 6 1/2" leaf strip.

7. Center the strip on the light triangle. Pin in place.

8. Set your machine with the blind hem stitch on 1 1/2 stitch width. Use invisible thread on the top and regular thread in the bobbin. Loosen the top thread tension.

9. Edgestitch in place with invisible thread and a blind hem stitch.

10. Trim the strip even with the triangle from the wrong side.

11. Sew the two triangles together. Trim the tips.

Sewing the Block Together

1. Arrange the pieces in this order:

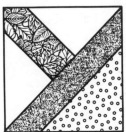

Sew together, matching the seams and outside edges.

3. Square up to 12 1/2".

Cactus Flower is the first block in the first row.

2. Arrange the remaining pieces in this order:

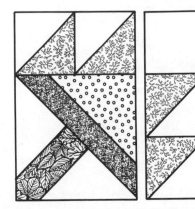

Quick Turn Finish

Beginning to Sew the Quilt Top Together for a Quick Turn Finish

1. Lay out Cactus Flower with two side triangles and one corner triangle.

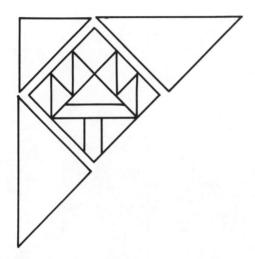

2. Flip the side triangles right sides together to the block. Pin, allowing a 1/4" tip to hang over on the top of the triangles and matching the square bottoms.

3. Stitch. Fold out the side triangles.

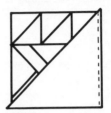

4. Flip the corner triangle right sides together to the block. Pin, allowing a 1/4" tip to extend on both ends.

5. Stitch.

6. Set aside until the second diagonal row is sewn.

As each block is completed, sew into a diagonal row. See the illustration on page 8 to see how the blocks are sewn together with the side triangles, corner triangles, and solid squares. Then sew the diagonal rows together into one top. After the borders and backing are sewn to the quilt top, "quick turn" the batting into the inside of the quilt in one piece.

1 Cactus Flower	3 Flower Basket	6 Patchwork Posy
2 Basket of Scraps	5 Cherry Basket	9 Carolina Lily
4 English Ivy	8 Pine Tree	11 Dobbins Fan
7 Star Basket	10 Tulip	12 Patch Blossoms

Machine Quilted Finish

Marking the Piece of Lightweight Bonded Batting

1. Cut the batting to the exact size of 68" x 85".

2. Spread the batting out flat on a large table and clamp in place, or tape to a large floor area.

3. Mark the following lines on the batting with a permanent marking pen. Use a yardstick, a 6" x 24" ruler and a Square Up for your measurements. A straight 8' long 1" x 2" furring strip is handy when marking long diagonal lines.

- a diagonal line drawn between two points 43" in on the upper left corner

- a light line 8" in on all four sides for approximate placement of borders

- four diagonal rows 12" wide (seam allowance is not included in batting)

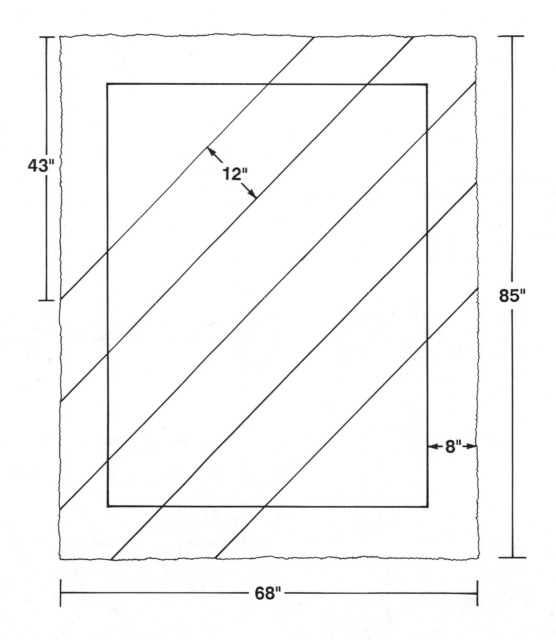

Machine Quilting the Blocks to the Bonded Batting in Diagonal Rows

Leave the lightweight bonded batting in one large piece and cut off each diagonal row of batting as you need it.

1. Lay the upper left corner of the bonded batting on the gridded cutting mat.

2. Cut on the diagonal line drawn between the 43" marks.

3. Place the block on the bottom center of the batting. Let the edge of the block hang over 1/4". Pin in place. To make the batting more manageable, roll in the corners and safety pin in place.

4. Thread your machine with lightweight nylon spun invisible thread. Loosen your top tension, and lengthen your stitch to 8-10 stitches per inch.

5. Load your bobbin with neutral sewing thread.

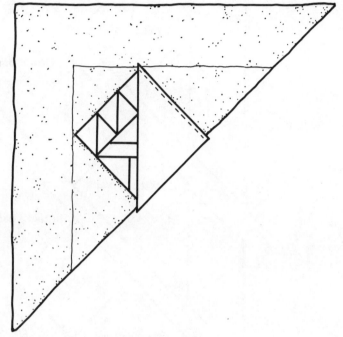

6. Place the needle in the depth of the seam by the dot, and "stitch in the ditch" around the dark triangles, across the green leaf, and around the medium triangle, following the arrows. Stitch continuously without removing the block from the machine, pivoting with the needle in the fabric at the points.

7. Place a side triangle right sides together to the Cactus Flower. Pin through all thicknesses, allowing a 1/4" tip to hang over on the top of the triangle and matching the square bottoms.

8. Stitch through all thicknesses, and fold back.

9. Stitch a side triangle to the opposite side of the block in the same manner.

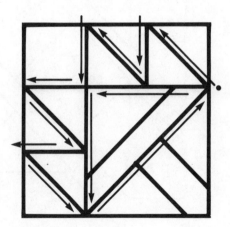

10. Place the corner triangle right sides together to the block. Pin, allowing a 1/4" tip to extend on both ends.

11. Stitch. Fold up.

12. Set aside until the next diagonal row is completed.

All Diagonal Rows of Finished Quilt

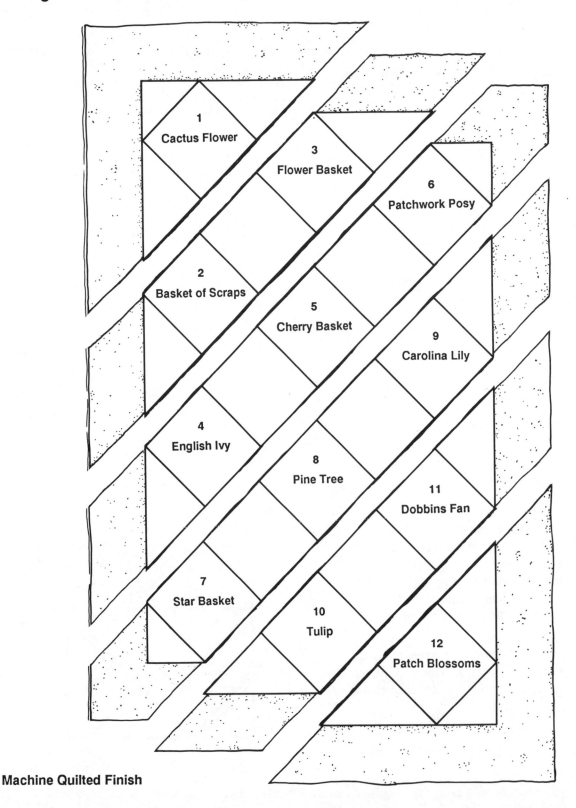

Machine Quilted Finish

Do not trim away the excess batting. An additional 8" of batting is allowed around all outside edges for the borders. Cut the batting into 12" wide diagonal rows as you complete the blocks and are ready for the next row. Follow the illustration when sewing the blocks together with the side triangles, corner triangles, and solid squares.

After all the blocks have been sewn in diagonal rows, the rows are flipped right sides together and stitched, being careful not to catch the batting in the seam. The batting is then butted and machine zigzagged or hand whipstitched together. After the backing is layered on the bottom, the borders are added through all layers, and the quilt is finished with a straight piece binding.

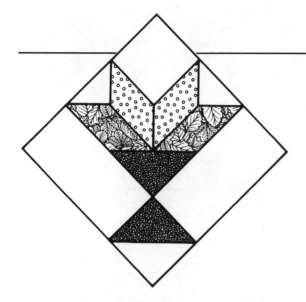

Basket of Scraps

As pioneer families made their journey westward in the 1800's, fabric that was once readily available on the East coast became a scarce commodity. Thus each quilt created by the pioneer woman was a work of art created out of the scrap bag or basket! Only on occasion were these precious scraps teamed with a new piece of cloth. Scrap bags held such importance that they were passed down from generation to generation, and often "willed" to a special friend or relative.

Choose one light background, one flower color, one leaf color, and one basket color.

Cutting Instructions

Layer Cut with Right Sides Together:

(1) 2 5/8" x 16" medium flower color
(1) 2 5/8" x 16" medium or dark leaf color

(1) 5" square basket color

(1) 4 5/8" square light background color
(1) 5 1/2" square light background color
(2) 4 1/2" x 8 1/2" light background color

Use a full and accurate 1/4" seam allowance and 15 stitches per inch. Use a 6" x 12" ruler or 6" x 24" ruler with a 45° line.

Sewing the Two

1. With the 2 5/8" x 16" flower and leaf strips right sides together, sew the length of the strips.

2. Cut into (2) 8" strips. Layer with the flower color on top on one strip, and the leaf color on top on the other strip.

3. On the left end, line up the 45° line on the ruler with the top of the strips. Trim.

4. Slide the ruler over, keeping the 45° line on the top of the strip. Match the 3 3/8" line on the ruler to the edge of the diagonal cut on the strip. Layer cut one segment from each strip.

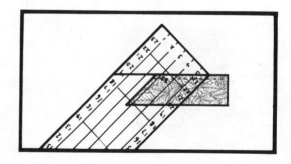

5. Carefully press the seams to the leaf color. Cut off the tips.

6. Lay them out in this order with the flower pieces next to each other:

7. Flip the piece on the right to the piece on the left. Match the seam and sew together, ending 1/4" from the edge. Press the seam to one side.

Inserting the 4 5/8" Light Square into the Corner of the Flower

1. From the wrong side of the square, mark a dot 1/4" from one corner with a pencil.
2. Flip up the top pair of flower and leaf to expose the seam allowance 1/4" from the end.
3. Matching the pencil mark to the 1/4" seam, sew from the mark out to the outside edge.
4. Flip to the second side and sew from the mark out.

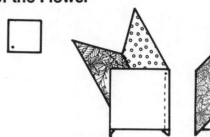

Inserting the Triangles into the Flower and Leaf

1. Cut the 5 1/2" light square into **three pieces:**
   Set aside the largest triangle for later.
2. Mark a dot 1/4" in on the corner on the wrong sides of the two small triangles.
3. Fold back and gently rip out 1/4" of stitches at the points between each flower and leaf.
4. Insert the triangles as the square was inserted.

Adding the Top of the Basket

1. Cut the 5" square basket color in half on the diagonal.
2. Sew one triangle to the bottom, allowing a 1/4" tip to hang over on each end.
3. Press the seam to the dark side.
4. Square up to 8 1/2", lining up the 8 1/2" mark on the Square Up to the corner of the basket triangle. Allow for the 1/4" seam when trimming.

Adding the Bottom of the Basket

1. Sew one 4 1/2" x 8 1/2" strip to the side of the basket.

2. Place the remaining large light triangle right sides together to the remaining basket triangle. **Note they are not the same size!**
3. Stitch. Trim the light to match the dark.

4. Sew to the end of one light 4 1/2 x 8 1/2 strip. Press the seam to the dark side.
5. Sew this last piece to the block, carefully matching the point. Square up to 12 1/2".

Basket of Scraps is the first block in the second diagonal row. Refer to page 8 to see how the row is sewn together.

(Optional) Machine Quilted Finish - Refer to page 7

1. From the large piece of bonded batting, cut off a row 12" wide.
2. Place a side triangle right side up 8" in from the left edge. Pin in place.
3. Flip the Basket of Scraps block right sides together to the side triangle.
4. Sew together through all layers. Fold back and flat.
5. Pin and sew a solid square to Basket of Scraps.
6. Machine quilt around Basket of Scraps, outlining the flower, leaf, and basket. If you wish, outline the large floral print in the solid square. See page 6 for more detail.

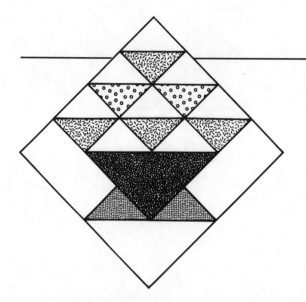

Flower Basket

Not only was her flower garden a thing of beauty to the pioneer woman, but her flowers also supplied her with all the materials necessary for dying her precious quilting fabrics. Right at her doorstep, she had lily-of-the-valley or Queen Anne's lace for a delicate yellow, marigolds for a deep orange, hollyhocks for red, and larkspur for blue and indigo. Dying was time-consuming, and sometimes disappointing. Cloth made under such circumstances was something to be cherished!

Choose one light background, two medium flower colors, and two basket colors.

Cutting Instructions

Layer Cut with Right Sides Together:

(1) 4" square light background
(1) 4" square first flower color

(1) 4" x 8" light background
(1) 4" x 8" second flower color

Cut in Half on Diagonal:

(1) 4" square light background
(1) 7" square light background
(1) 7" square medium basket color
(1) 4" square dark basket color

(2) 3 5/8" x 6 1/2" light background

Use a full and accurate 1/4" seam allowance and 15 stitches per inch.

Sewing the

1. With the 4" x 8" rectangles of light and flower color right sides together, draw on a 4" square line.

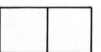

2. Draw on diagonal lines on this piece and the 4" square of light and flower color right sides together.

3. Sew a 1/4" seam on both sides of the diagonal lines. Press.

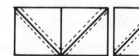

4. Cut apart on all lines.

5. Press the seams to the darker sides.

6. Trim off the tips.

7. Lay out with the two light triangles made from cutting the 4" square light on the diagonal in this order:

8. Flip the second vertical row right sides together to the first row.

9. Assembly line sew the first vertical row.

10. Flip the third vertical row right sides together to the second row.

11. Assembly line sew.

12. Sew the horizontal rows.

13. If necessary, straighten the bottom edge, leaving a 1/4" seam.

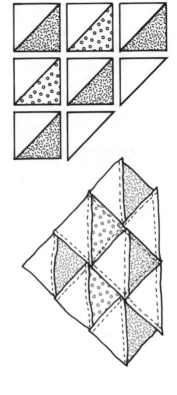

Sewing the

1. Place the large triangle medium basket color right sides together to the flower patchwork. Let a 1/4" tip extend over on each end.

2. Sew with the flower patchwork on top.

3. Square up to 9 1/2".

Adding the Feet to the Basket

1. Sew small dark basket triangles to the light 3 5/8" x 6 1/2" strips in this order:

Match the straight edges. Allow a 1/4" tip to hang over.

2. Sew the left foot to the basket. Open out.

3. Sew the right foot to the basket. Open out.

4. Sew the large light triangle to the bottom of the basket with the patchwork on the top.

5. Square up to 12 1/2".

Flower Basket is the second block in the first horizontal row. Refer to page 8 for block placement.

(Optional) Machine Quilted Finish - Refer to page 7.

1. Lay out the 12" wide row of bonded batting cut in the previous Block Party. A side triangle, Basket of Scraps, and a solid square are already sewn to this diagonal row.

2. Pin the Flower Basket block right sides together to the solid square through the batting.

3. Sew together through all layers. Fold back and flat.

4. Machine quilt around the basket and flowers.

5. Pin a side triangle right sides together to the Flower Basket block.

6. Sew through all layers. Fold out flat.

7. If you wish, outline the floral print in the solid square with invisible thread.

This completes the second diagonal row. Flip the second row right sides together to the first row. Match, pin, and sew only the blocks together. Do not include the batting in the stitches. Butt the batting together. Hand whipstitch or machine zig zag stitch the batting together.

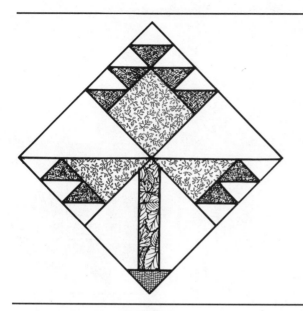

English Ivy

Typical of older quilt patterns, English Ivy is simply composed of triangles and squares. This climbing vine with its woody stem and evergreen leaves covered the shaded brick walls of the New Englanders' homes . The ivy offered ornamentation to the home, as well as shade to the quilter, a welcomed relief on a hot summer day!

When creating the look of ivy plant colors, select one light background, two leaf colors, and two basket colors, particularly if the basket colors are brown.When creating the look of a flower with color, select one light background, two flower colors, and two leaf or stem colors.

Cutting Instructions

Layer Cut with Right Sides Together:
(1) 6" x 9" piece light background
(1) 6" x 9" piece dark leaf or flower color

(1) 4 5/8" square medium leaf or flower color
(1) 6 1/2" square light background
(1) 1 1/2" x 8 1/2" strip leaf or basket color

Cut in Half on Diagonal:
(1) 5" square medium leaf or flower color
(1) 7" square light background
(1) 3" square leaf or basket color

Use a full and accurate 1/4" seam allowance and 15 stitches per inch.

Sewing the

1. Draw a 3" grid on the 6" x 9" pieces.

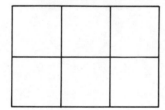

3. Draw on diagonal lines the opposite way every other row.

4. Cut out one 3" square and cut on the diagonal. Set aside.

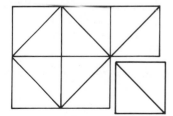

2. Draw on diagonal lines every other row.

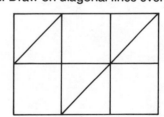

5. Continuously sew a 1/4" seam on both sides of the diagonal lines. Press.

6. Cut apart. Press the seams to the dark side.

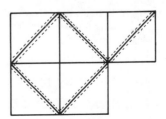

7. Arrange two sets of each in this order:

   Assembly line sew.

8. Add the two light triangles cut from the 3"
   squares in this order to one set of each:

9. Add another pieced triangle to one set:

Making the

1. Lay out the pieces in this order with the 4 5/8" medium square:

2. Sew on the shortest piece first.

3. Sew on the longer piece, matching the seam.

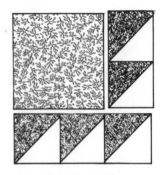

Making the

1. Lay out the pieces in this order with the two medium triangles cut from
   the 5" square; match up the straight edges.

2. Sew on each piece.

3. Lay out with the two light triangles cut from the 7" square

4. Sew on each piece, matching the outside edges of
   the triangles.

   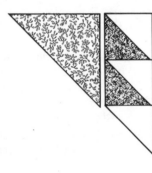

Making the

1. Press under the raw edges of the 1 1/2" x 8 1/2" leaf or basket color strip.

2. Pin on the diagonal down the center of the 6 1/2" light square.

3. Edgestitch. *(You may use a blind hem stitch and invisible thread.)*

4. Place one triangle cut from the 3" leaf or basket square right sides together to the
   light corner, 2 1/2" up on each side from the corner.

5. Stitch. Press down and flat.

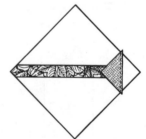

Sewing the Block Together

1. Square up each piece to 6 1/2".

2. Lay out in order and sew together.

English Ivy is the first block in the third diagonal row. Refer to page 8 for block placement.

(Optional) Machine Quilted Finish - Refer to page 7.

1. From the large piece of bonded batting, cut off a new row 12" wide.

2. Place a side triangle right side up 8" in from the left edge. Pin in place.

3. Flip the English Ivy block right sides together to the side triangle.

4. Sew together through all layers. Fold back and flat.

5. Continuously machine quilt around English Ivy, beginning on one side of the stem, and ending on the other side.

6. Pin and sew a solid square to English Ivy. Outline the large floral print.

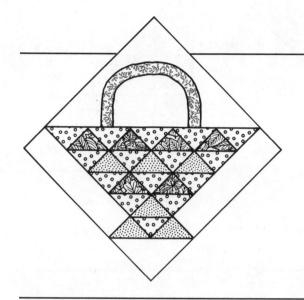

Cherry Basket

Baskets are common containers around Amish farms. Carrying produce from garden to house or from garden to market is often done in baskets. The adoption of this pattern by Amish women is somewhat unusual, as Amish quilts tend to avoid the realistic reproductions of an object. The bottom part of the Cherry Basket is pieced; the handle is appliqued.

Choose one light background, two mediums, and two darks from any of the basket and flower colors.

Cutting Instructions

Layer Cut with Right Sides Together for Basket:

(1) 3" x 6" first medium color
(1) 3" x 6" first dark color

(1) 3" x 9" first medium color
(1) 3" x 9" second dark color

(2) 6" x 8 1/2" second medium color for handle

(2) 8 3/4" x 2 5/8" light background strips

Cut in half on diagonal for basket:

(3) 3" squares first medium color
(1) 3" first dark color

(1) 11" square light background (Only half of square cut on diagonal is needed. From remaining half, cut next square.)

(1) 5" square light background

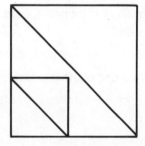

Use a full and accurate 1/4" seam allowance and 15 stitches per inch.

Making the

1. With the 3" x 6" pieces and 3" x 9" pieces right sides together, draw on 3" square lines.

2. Draw on diagonal lines.

3. Sew a 1/4" seam on both sides of the diagonal lines. Press.

4. Cut apart on all lines.

5. Press the seams to the darker side.

6. Trim off the tips.

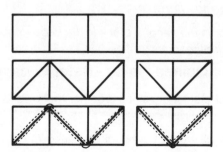

7. Line up these pieces and the triangles cut from the 3" medium squares in this order:

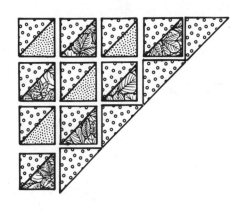 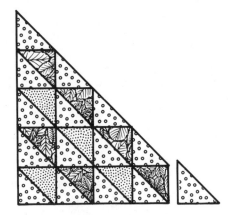

8. Sew in the vertical rows, allowing a 1/4" tip to hang over on each of the medium triangles.

9. Sew in the horizontal rows.

10. Add a medium triangle to one side.

11. Press flat.

12. Straighten the edges. Do not trim off the 1/4" seam allowances.

Adding the

1. Sew a triangle cut from the 3" first dark square to the ends of the 8 3/4" x 2 5/8" light strips in this order:

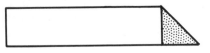 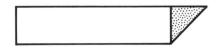

2. Sew to the basket, one at a time, from the triangles out. Allow the tip on the triangle to hang over, and match the seam to the basket. The light strip is shorter than the basket.

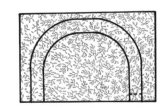

Making the Handle

1. *(Optional - Stabilize the paper pattern to a piece of cardboard with iron-on webbed fusing.)* Cut out the handle pattern.

2. Trace the pattern onto the 6" x 8 1/2" pieces of second medium.

3. Stitch on the traced line. Leave one short end open. On the opposite end, sew a line of stitching 1/2" from the end.

4. Trim to within 1/16" from the stitched line. Do not trim off the stitched end.

5. Insert a pencil eraser into the stitched end of the handle.

6. By pressing the pencil on the end, turn the handle right side out.

7. Press flat.

8. Evenly position the handle on the triangle cut from the 11" light square. Line the handle up with the basket bottom. Pin in place.

9. Stitch around the handle with invisible thread and a blind hem stitch.

10. Sew on the 5" square cut on the diagonal to the bottom of the basket.

11. Square up the block to 12 1/2".

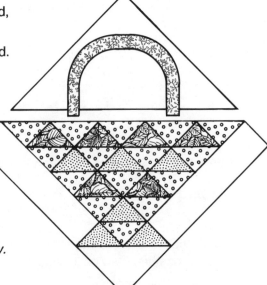

The Cherry Basket block is the second block in the second horizontal row. Refer to page 8 for block placement.

(Optional) Machine Quilted Finish - Refer to page 7.

1. Flip the Cherry Basket block right sides together to the solid square block in the third diagonal row of bonded batting. Pin.

2. Sew together through all layers. Fold back and flat.

3. Continuously machine quilt around Cherry Basket.

4. Pin and sew a solid square to Cherry Basket. Outline the large floral print.

Cherry Basket

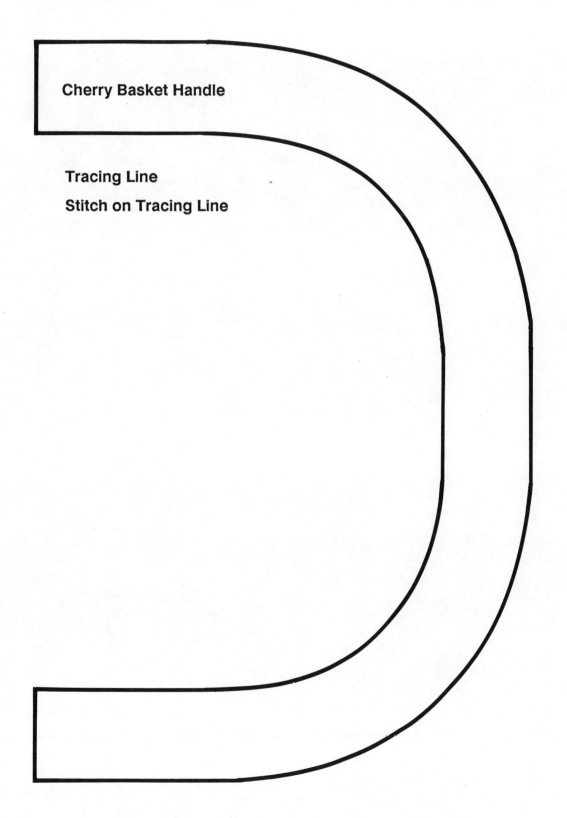

Cherry Basket Handle

Tracing Line

Stitch on Tracing Line

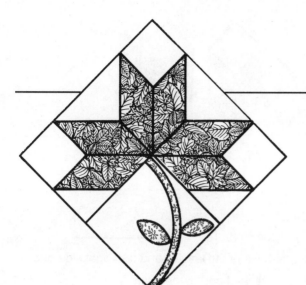

Patchwork Posy

Nature has inspired many quilt patterns, as the Patchwork Posy, which features diamonds in its design. Perhaps good friends gathered around a quilting frame, shared the news in their lives, and were inspired to design the Patchwork Posy. They realized flowers are just like people - they are nice companions.

Choose a light background color, one flower color, and a leaf color.

Cutting Instructions

(1) 2 5/8" x 45" strip flower color

(2) 4" x 9" squares leaf color

(3) 3 3/4" squares light background
(1) 4" square light background
(1) 6 5/8" square light background
(1) 7 1/4" square light background

Use a full and accurate 1/4" seam allowance and 15 stitches per inch.

Use a 6" x 12" ruler or 6" x 24" ruler with 45° line.

Making the Posy

1. Cut the flower color strip in half. Place right sides together, and sew.

2. On the left end, line up the 45° line on the top of the strip. Trim. Discard.

3. Slide the ruler over, keeping the 45° line on the top of the strip. Line up the diagonal cut with the 3 5/8" line. Cut. Continue to cut a total of three diamonds in this manner.

4. Open, and press the seams to one side.

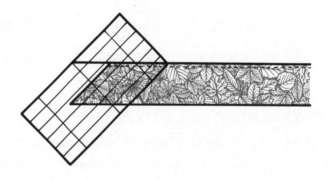

Sewing in the Light Corners

1. Remove a 1/4" of stitches from the corner of each diamond.

2. With a marking pencil, place a dot 1/4" in one corner of each 3 3/4" square.

3. At one corner of the diamond, right sides together, pin the 1/4" open seam of the diamond with the dot on the square.

4. Stitch to the outside edge.

5. Swing the square to meet the diamond edge and sew from the dot to the point.

6. Repeat with the other two diamonds. Press the seams to the dark side.

7. Cut the 4" square in half of the diagonal. Sew to two of the diamonds, allowing a 1/4" tip to hang over on each end.

8. Placing the 45° line down the center of the diamond, square up to 6 5/8".

Machine Stitching the Stem and Leaf

1. Cut out the paper patterns. Trace two leaves and one stem on the leaf fabric, with the pieces of fabric right sides together.

2. Stitch on the pencil line around the leaves. Leave one end open on the stem.

3. Trim to within 1/16" of the pencil line. Make a small cut in the center back of the leaves, and turn right side out.

4. Turn the stem right side out by inserting the tip of an eraser into the stitched end of the stem.

5. Press flat. Pin in place on the 6 5/8" light square.

6. Outline stitch with invisible thread and the blind hem stitch.

Sewing the Block Together

1. Lay out the four pieces in this order:

2. Seam the vertical row, and then the horizontal row. Leave the two seams open 1/4" where the triangles are inserted.

Inserting the Triangles

1. Cut the 7 1/4" light square in fourths on the diagonals. Discard two of the triangles.

2. With a marking pencil, place a dot in the corner of the triangle 1/4" in from the outside edge.

3. Working on one side at a time, sew in the triangles, stitching from the 1/4" dot to the outside edges.

4. Square up the block to 12 1/2".

Patchwork Posy is the third block in the first horizontal row. Refer to page 8 for block placement.

(Optional) Machine Quilted Finish - Refer to page 7.

1. Flip Patchwork Posy block right sides together to the solid square block in the third diagonal row of bonded batting. Pin.

2. Sew together through all thicknesses. Fold back and flat.

3. Continuously machine quilt around Patchwork Posy.

4. Pin and sew a corner triangle to the end of the row.

This completes the third diagonal row. Flip the third row right sides together to the second row. Match, pin, and sew only the blocks together . Do not include the batting in the stitches. Hand whipstitch the batting or machine zigzag stitch to the second diagonal row.

Patchwork Posy

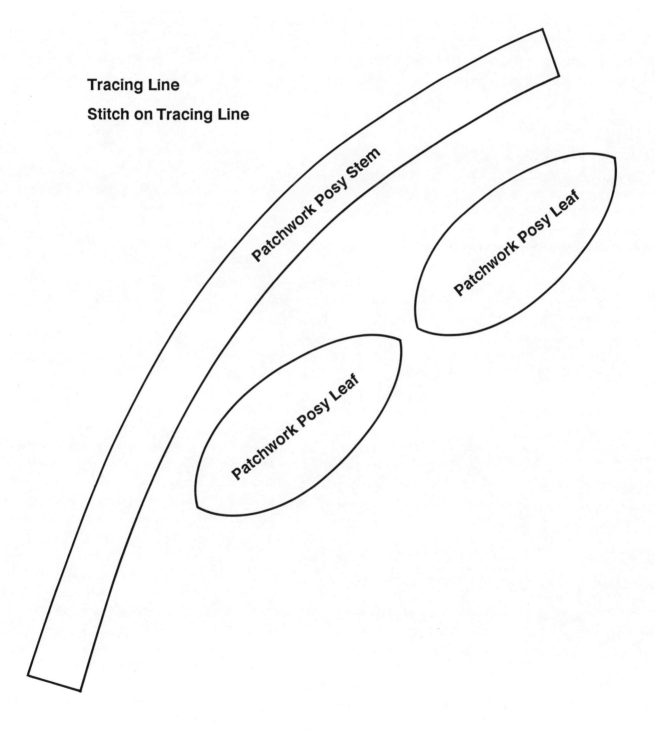

Tracing Line

Stitch on Tracing Line

Patchwork Posy Stem

Patchwork Posy Leaf

Patchwork Posy Leaf

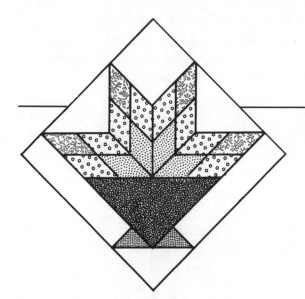

Star Basket

First popularized around 1910, the Star Basket is also identified as Flower Pot, Calico Bush, Cactus Basket, and Tulip Basket. Baskets, popular in general society, were common containers around farms.

Choose one light background color, two mediums and a dark from any of the flowers or leaves colors, and two basket colors.

Cutting Instructions

Layer Cut for the Flowers:
(1) 1 7/8" x 18" dark flower or leaf
(1) 1 7/8" x 18" first medium flower or leaf
(2) 1 7/8" x 18" second medium flower or leaf

Cut in Half on Diagonal for Basket:
(1) 6 3/4" square first basket color
(1) 3 1/4" square second basket color

Cut for the Background:
(1) 4 3/4" square light background
(1) 7 1/2" square light background
(2) 3" x 7 3/4" strips light background

Use a full and accurate 1/4" seam allowance and 15 stitches per inch.
Use a 6" x 12" or 6" x 24" ruler with a 45° line.

Making the Diamonds

1. Place a dark and second medium strip right sides together. Place a first and second medium strip right sides together.

2. Sew the length of the strips. On the dark/second medium strip, press the seams toward the dark. On the first medium/second medium strip, press the seams toward the second medium. Layer the two sets of strips on top of each other.

3. Line up the 45° line on the top left end of the strips. Trim on the 45° angle. Discard.

4. Slide the ruler to the right. Line up the diagonal cut with the 1 7/8" line, and the 45° line with the top of the strips. Cut.

5. Continue to cut a total of four diamonds per strip in this manner.

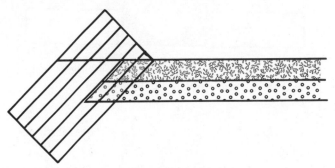

6. Divide into two equal piles, with four in each.

7. Flip the strip on the right onto the strip on the left. Match, pin, and stitch all four. Press the seams to the dark/medium.

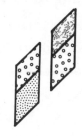

8. Divide into two equal piles, with two in each.

9. Sew the diamonds together from the center point out to 1/4" from the edge.

10. Press. Square up using the end of the ruler.

11. Stitch the two together, matching the center seams and ending 1/4" from the end. Straighten if necessary. Do not trim away the 1/4" seam allowance.

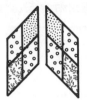  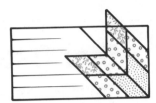 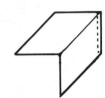

Adding the Basket

1. Pin the triangle cut from the 6 3/4" first basket color to the bottom of the diamonds. Allow tips to extend equally on each end.

2. Stitch. Press away from the diamonds.

Sewing in the Light Corner

1. With a marking pencil, place a dot 1/4" in on one corner.

2. Pin the 1/4" open seam of the diamond with the dot on the square. Stitch to the outside edge.

3. Swing the square to meet the opposite diamond edge, and sew from the dot to the outside edge.

4. Press the seam toward the diamonds.

Sewing in the Light Triangles

1. Cut the 7 1/2" square into thirds.

2. Place a dot in the corners of the two smaller triangles 1/4" in from the outside edges.

3. Sew the triangles into the sides of the diamonds, stitching from the 1/4" dot to the outside edges.

4. Square up the partial block to 10".

Sewing on the Side Strips and Bottom

1. Sew the triangles cut from the second basket color to each end of the 3" x 7 3/4" light strips.

2. Sew to the basket, one at a time, from the triangles out. Allow the tip on the triangles to hang over.

3. Trim 1" from the large triangle left over from the 7 1/2" square.

4. Sew to the bottom of the basket.

5. Square up the block to 12 1/2", allowing a 1/4" seam allowance to remain on all four sides.

Star Basket block is the first block in the fourth diagonal row. Refer to page 8 for block placement

(Optional) Machine Quilted Finish - Refer to page 7.

1. From the large piece of bonded batting, cut off a row 12" wide.

2. Place a corner triangle right side up 8" in on the bottom left corner. Pin in place.

3. Flip the Star Basket block right sides together to the corner triangle.

4. Sew together through all layers. Fold back and flat.

5. Continuously machine quilt around the block, outlining the outside edge.

6. Pin and sew a solid square to Star Basket. Outline the large floral print.

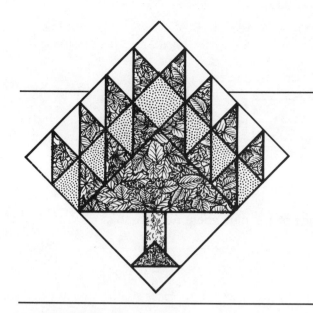

Pine Tree

The Pine Tree, also identified as the Temperance Tree, is recognized as one of the oldest quilt patterns known in the United States. It was used in colonial New England on coins and flags as a symbol of freedom in a rich new land. The name of the block was unchanged through the massive pioneer migrations that settled this country.

Choose one light background, medium basket or flower color, dark leaf color, and a dark basket color.

Cutting Instructions

Layer Cut with Right Sides Together:
Branches
(1) 7" square light background
(1) 7" square dark leaf color

(1) 7" square medium color
(1) 7" square dark leaf color

(1) 3" square light background
(1) 3" square medium color

Base of Tree
(1) 8 1/4" square light background
(1) 8 1/4" square dark leaf color

Trunk
(1) 2 1/4" x 4" dark basket color
(1) 3" square dark basket color

Except where specified, use a full and accurate 1/4" seam allowance and 15 stitches per inch.

Sewing the Eight and Eight

1. With the two sets of 7" squares right sides together, draw on 3 1/2" square lines.

2. Draw on diagonal lines.

3. Sew a 1/4" seam on both sides of the diagonal lines. Press.

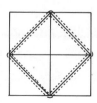

4. Cut apart on all lines.

5. Press the seams to the dark side. Square up each to 3".

6. Arrange two groups in this order, including the 3" light and 3" medium squares.

 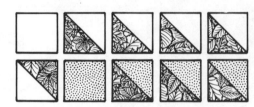

Sew these 3" units together using a generous seam allowance of 1/4" plus about two threads.

7. Sew in the vertical rows. Sew in the horizontal rows. Press.

Making the

1. Cut the 8 1/4" squares of light and dark in half on the diagonal. Discard one of each.

2. Press under 1/4" raw edges on the 2 1/4" x 4" dark trunk. Center on the light triangle. Pin in place.

3. Fold the 3" dark square in half on the diagonal with right sides together. Sew around the outside edge. Trim the seam. Clip a hole in the center back. Turn right side out. Press.

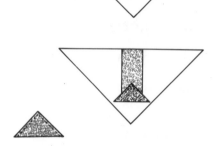

4. Layer on top of the trunk bottom edge, leaving 1/4" of background for seam allowance. Pin in place.

The trunk may be edge stitched or blind hem appliqued now or when the block is machine quilted.

5. Place the light and dark triangles right sides together. Sew.

Sewing the Block Together

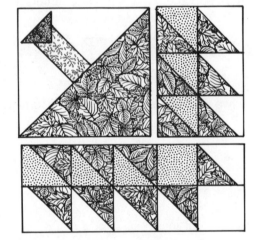

1. Arrange the pieces in this order:

2. Sew the shorter piece of branches to the trunk first. **Use a generous 1/4" seam.** Fold out flat.

3. Sew on the longer piece using the same generous seam allowance, matching the seams.

4. Square up to 12 1/2" as closely as you can without trimming the seam allowance off the points.

Pine Tree is the second block in the third horizontal row. Refer to page 8 for block placement.

(Optional) Machine Quilted Finish - Refer to page 7.

1. Flip the Pine Tree block right sides together to the solid square block in the fourth diagonal row of bonded batting. Pin

2. Sew together through all layers. Fold back and flat.

3. Machine quilt around Pine Tree.

4. Pin and sew a solid square to Pine Tree. Outline the large floral print.

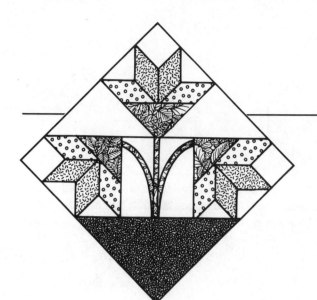

Carolina Lily

The lily was a very popular design motif in mid nineteenth century quilts, and the pattern acquired many different names as it traveled across the country. It was called Wood Lily in northern New England, Meadow Lily in Pennsylvania, North Carolina Lily throughout the South, and Mountain Lily in Kentucky and Tennessee.

Choose one light background, two flower colors, one leaf color, and one basket color.

Cutting Instructions

Layer Cut with Right Sides Together:

(2) 2 1/8" x 12" first flower color
(2) 2 1/8" x 12" second flower color

(3) 2 3/4" light squares
(2) 4 1/2" light squares
(1) 6" light square
(1) 4 5/8" x 5 1/2" light rectangle

(2) 4" squares leaf color
(1) 1 1/2" x 22" strip leaf color

(1) 8" square basket color

Use a full and accurate 1/4" seam allowance and 15 stitches per inch. Use a ruler with a 45° line.

Sewing the Flowers

1. Place the 2 1/8" x 12" flower strips right sides together.

2. Sew the first set with the first flower color on top.

3. Sew the second set with the second flower color on top.

4. Layer the strips on top of each other.

5. Lay the ruler with the 45° line across the top of the strips.

6. Cut on the 45° angle. Keeping the 45° line on the top of the strip, slide the ruler along and cut (3) 2 1/8" segments from each strip.

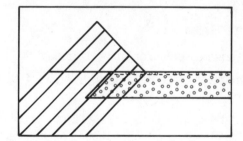

7. Open and press the seams toward the darker flower color. Trim off the tips.

8. Lay out two stacks of three each in your preferred color arrangement.

9. Assembly line sew to within 1/4" from the end of each pair. Press the seams to one side.

Inserting the 2 3/4" Light Squares into the Flowers

1. From the wrong side of the squares, mark a dot 1/4" from one corner with a pencil.

2. Lay the pieces out in this order:

3. Expose the 1/4" seam allowance next to the corner of each marked square by gently removing 1/4" of stitches on two as you open them.

4. Matching the pencil mark to the 1/4" exposed seam, sew to the outside edges of each square. Press the seams away from the square.

Inserting the Remaining Triangles

1. Cut the (2) 4 1/2" squares into fourths on the diagonals. Mark a dot 1/4" in on the wrong side of each triangle.

2. Lay the pieces out in this order:

3. Fold back and gently rip out 1/4" of stitches at the points of each.

4. Insert the triangles as the squares were inserted. Press away from the triangles.

Adding the Base

1. Cut (2) 4" squares leaf color on the diagonals.

2. Sew the triangles to the bottoms, allowing a 1/4" tip to hang over on each end. Press.

3. Square up the square piece to 5 1/2". Straighten the sides of the other two without trimming off the seam allowance.

Adding the Light Triangles

1. Cut the (1) 6" light square in half on the diagonal.

2. Sew it to the square flower. Match the straight top edges. Allow a 1/4" tip to hang over at the center.

Making the Stems

1. Tie a knot on the end of a 25" long piece of strong cording.

2. Place the cording down the center of the 1 1/2" x 22" leaf strip, with the knot at the top.

3. Fold the strip in half right sides together over the cord.

4. Backstitch across the top and sew downs the side. Do not catch the cord on the side.

5. Pull the cord and turn right side out. Press.

6. Cut into three equal pieces.

7. Pin in place on the 4 5/8" x 5 1/2" light in this arrangement:

8. Blind hem stitch with invisible thread now or when you machine quilt.

9. Sew the two flowers onto each side.

Sewing the Block Together

1. Cut the (1) 8" basket color in half on the diagonal. Discard one half.

2. Lay the pieces out in this order. Pin the center of the top flower to the center of the stem.

3. Sew together.

4. Square up to 12 1/2" as closely as you can without trimming off any seam allowances.

Carolina Lily is the third block in the second horizontal row. Refer to page 8 for block placement.

(Optional) Machine Quilted Finish - Refer to page 7.

1. Flip the block right sides together to the solid square block in the fourth diagonal row of bonded batting. Pin.

2. Sew together through all layers. Fold back and flat.

3. Machine quilt around the flowers.

4. Pin and sew a side triangle to the block. Outline the large floral print.

This completes the fourth diagonal row. Sew blocks in the fourth diagonal row to the third diagonal row being careful not to catch the batting. Hand whipstitch the batting or machine zigzag stitch to the third diagonal row.

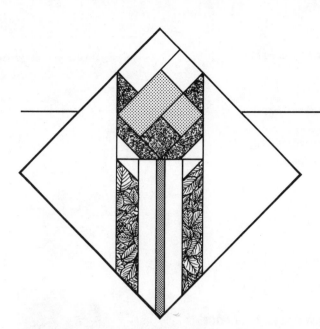

Tulip

Among the flowers that are featured in quilts, the tulip is one of the most popular. Most often the patterns were appliqued. This is a pieced tulip featured in Ruby McKim's book, *101 Patchwork Patterns*. It can be set together without the large triangles on each side, like a diamond paned window with white blocks the same size. Turn the tulip into a rectangle by adding corner colored triangles.

Choose a light background, a medium and a dark flower color, and two leaf colors.

Cutting Instructions:

Layer Cut Flower Section:
(1) 2 1/2" x 4 1/2" light background
(1) 2 1/2" x 4 1/2" medium flower color

(1) 2 1/2" square light background color
(1) 2 1/2" square medium flower color
(1) 2 1/2" square dark flower color

Layer Cut with Right Sides Together
(1) 1 1/2" x 10" dark flower color
(1) 1 1/2" x 10" light background

Stem and Leaf Section:
(2) 1 3/4" x 10" light background
(2) 1 3/4" x 8 1/2" green leaf color
(1) 1 1/4" x 10" green stem color

Cut on the Diagonal:
(1) 2 7/8" square dark flower color
(1) 2 1/4" square light background
(1) 9 1/2" square light background

Use a full and accurate 1/4" seam allowance and 15 stitches per inch.

Sewing the Flower in Three Rows

1. Arrange and assembly line sew:

Light rectangle and dark triangle
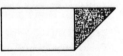

Medium rectangle and light square
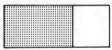

Dark square, medium square, and dark triangle
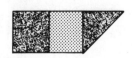

Press the seams to the dark side. Clip apart.

2. Lay out the three rows. Flip the middle row onto the first row making the top edges even. Sew. Turn the two sections around and flip them onto the third row matching the top edges and the one seam. Press the seams to one side.

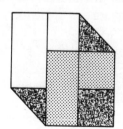

Adding the Base of the Flower

1. Sew the 1 1/2" x 10" light and dark flower pieces. Press seam to dark side. Cut into (2) 5" pieces.

2. Arrange a base piece next to the flower. Flip flower onto base, matching top edges. Sew the length of flower edge. Press seam toward base.

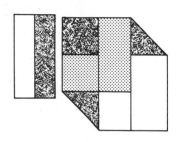

3. Lay Square Up ruler on flower with diagonal line on flower seams and ruler edge along triangle edge. There should be a seam allowance beyond the point of the dark square. Trim away the base edges.

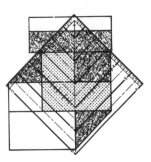

4. Center remaining base piece under other flower edge. Sew length of flower. Press toward base.

5. Lay Square Up ruler on flower with diagonal line on flower seams and ruler edge along triangle edge. There should be a seam allowance beyond the point of the dark square. Trim away the base edges.

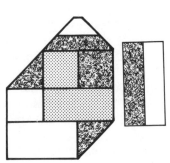

Sewing the Stem and Leaves Section

1. **Right sides together,** trim a 45° angle from one end of the (2) 1 3/4" x 8 1/2" leaves.

2. Sew a small light triangle to each of those ends. Press seam toward triangle. Trim tips and edges to square end of stems.

3. Lay out and sew stem and leaves section. Press seams toward dark fabrics.

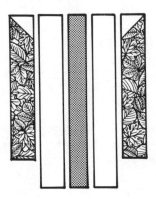

Sewing Together the Flower with the Stem and Leaves Section

1. Match center of flower to middle of stem. Sew the sections with the flower on top. Press seam toward flower.

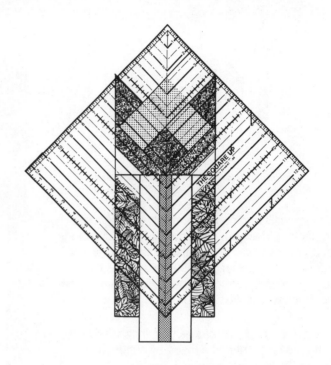

2. Lay Square Up on block with corner of ruler in flower corner and diagonal line down center of stem. Trim off excess stem and leaves.

Adding the Side Triangles

1. Sew triangles from 9 1/2" square to flower.

2. Press seams toward triangles. Square up to 12 1/2" *Tulip is the second block in the fourth horizontal row. Refer to page 8 for block placement.*

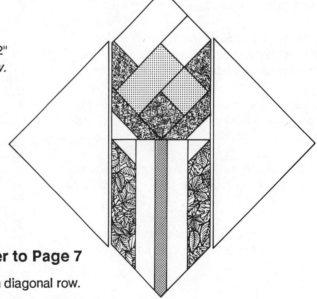

(Optional) Machine Quilted Finish - Refer to Page 7

1. From the piece on bonded batting, cut off the fifth diagonal row.

2. Place a side triangle right side up 8" up from the bottom edge. Pin in place.

3. Flip Tulip right sides together to the side triangle.

4. Sew together through all layers. Fold back and flat.

5. Continuously machine quilt around Tulip.

6. Pin and sew a solid square to Tulip. Outline the large floral print.

One Tulip Block or One Solid Rectangle

Approximate Finished Size: 5 1/4" x 16 1/4"

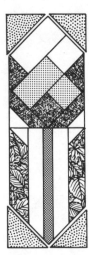 

Plan your wallhanging layout by alternating a rectangular tulip design plus corners with a solid block plus corners the same size, like a diamond paned window. In the wallhanging illustrated, there are five tulip blocks and four solid blocks. Traditionally, the solid block was white.

Make as many tulip blocks as you choose without adding the large triangles made by cutting the 9 1/2" squares on the diagonal.

Using the sewn together tulip as a pattern, cut out solid blocks the same size.

For every tulip block you make, cut (2) 3 1/2" squares medium color. Cut the squares on the diagonals, and sew one triangle to each corner.

Cut (2) 3 1/2" squares second medium color for each solid block. Cut them on the diagonal, and sew one to each corner.

Sew the blocks together in vertical rows, alternating the tulip and solid blocks. Sew in the horizontal rows.

Add 4 1/2" borders to the four sides. Finish the wallhanging with any of your favorite methods.

Tulip Wallhanging

Approximate Finished Size: 24" x 57"

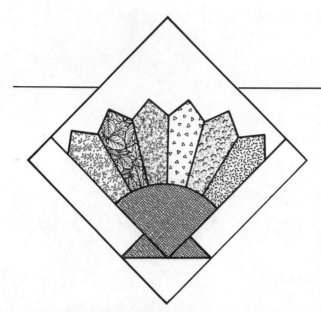

Dobbin's Fan

As is often the case with the names of quilt blocks, or anything else handed down by word of mouth, the origin of the name can sometimes be a mystery. Dobbin is a nickname for Robin. It is also a term used for a horse with a gentle gait and patient demeanor. From this we can logically assume that perhaps this block was designed with "Dobbin" in mind - be it a girl named Robin, or a gentle old horse.

Choose a light background, an assortment of six fan colors, and a dark basket.

Cutting Instructions

(1) 10 3/4" light background square
(2) 2 1/2" x 8 3/4" light background
(1) 4 3/4" light background square
(1) 5 1/2" x 13" light background

(2) 5" square dark basket
(1) 3" square dark basket

(6) 3" x 6 1/2" rectangles in color assortment

Use a full and accurate 1/4" seam allowance and 15 stitches per inch.

Making the Fan

1. Plan and lay out the color assortment of six rectangles.

2. Flip #2 onto #1. Flip #4 onto #3. Flip #6 onto #5.

3. Stack into one pile with #2 on top.

4. Cut out and lay fan pattern on #2 and layer cut.

5. Assembly line sew the wedges together.

6. From the wrong side with the curve on the top, press the seams to the left.

7. Pin fan right sides together to the 5 1/2" x 13" light background.

8. Sew 1/4" seam around the points of the fan, pivoting at the points with the needle in the fabric.

9. Trim to 1/16". Turn right side out.

10. Carefully push out the points and press flat.

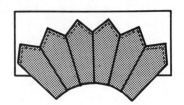

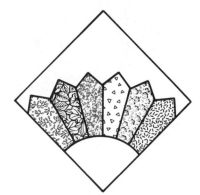

11. Layer onto the 10 3/4" light square, matching the outside raw edges. Pin in place.

Making the Basket

1. Cut out and place the basket template on the 5" basket squares with right sides together. Match the corner of the pattern with the corner of the fabric square.

2. Trace the curve. Sew on the traced curve.

3. Trim to 1/16" from the stitched line.

4. Turn right side out. Press. Layer onto the 10 3/4" square, matching the outside raw edges. Pin in place.

5. Blind hem stitch the fan wedges and basket to the background square now, or when you machine quilt later.

6. Sew the triangles cut from the 3" basket square to the 2 1/2" x 8 3/4" light background strips.

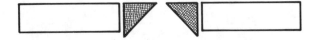

7. Sew to the fan.

8. Straighten the bottom edge, leaving the seam allowance.

9. Cut the 4 3/4" square on the diagonal. Sew the triangle to the bottom of the fan, allowing a 1/4" tip to hang over equally on each side.

10. Square up to 12 1/2" as closely as you can without trimming off any seam allowance.

Dobbin's Fan is the third block in the third horizontal row. Refer to page 8 for block placement.

(Optional) Machine Quilted Finish - Refer to page 7.

1. Flip the block right sides together to the solid square block in the fifth diagonal row of bonded batting. Pin.

2. Sew together through all thicknesses. Fold back and flat.

3. Machine quilt around the flowers.

4. Pin and sew a side triangle to the block. Outline the large floral print.

This completes the fifth diagonal row. Sew blocks in fifth diagonal row to fourth diagonal row being careful not to catch the batting. Hand whipstitch the batting or machine zig zag stitch to the fourth diagonal row.

Dobbin's Fan

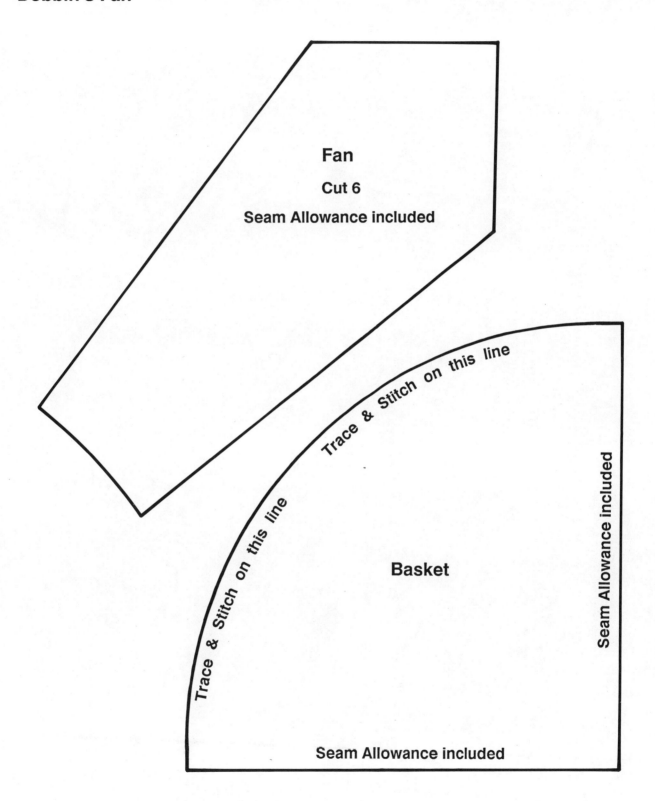

Fan

Cut 6

Seam Allowance included

Trace & Stitch on this line

Trace & Stitch on this line

Basket

Seam Allowance included

Seam Allowance included

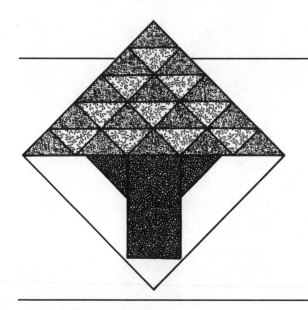

Patch Blossoms

Victorian women of the eighteenth century often took a "patchwork of blossoms" from their gardens as roses, lavender, and cornflowers, and layered them with herbs and spices in a container. Then natural fixatives such as orris-root, frankincense, and myrrh were added to absorb the fragrance and hold it for years.

Choose a light background, an assortment of five flower colors for a scrap look or one flower color for same color blossoms, a medium leaf color, and a dark stem color.

Cutting Instructions

Layer Cut with Right Sides Together:

(5) 3 1/2" squares assortment of flower colors for Scrap Blossoms or
(1) 3 1/2" x 17 1/2" flower color for Same Color Blossoms

(1) 13" square light background (Press in half and cut on diagonal. Discard one half)

(1) 3 1/2" x 17 1/2" medium leaf color
(3) 3 1/2" squares medium leaf color
(Cut in half on diagonals)

(1) 4" x 7 1/4" dark stem color
(1) 3 1/8" square dark stem
(Cut in half on diagonal)

Use a full and accurate 1/4" seam allowance except where specified and 15 stitches per inch.

Sewing the Ten

1. Scrap Blossoms: Draw diagonal lines on the (5) 3 1/2" squares. Same Color Blossoms: Draw on 3 1/2" square lines. Draw on diagonal lines.

2. Place right sides together to the 3 1/2" x 17 1/2" leaf strip.

3. Sew a 1/4" seam on both sides of the diagonal lines.

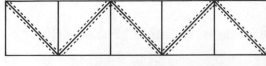
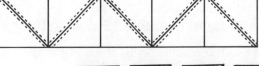

4. Cut apart on all lines.

5. Press the seams to the darker side.

6. Square up to 3".

7. Line up these pieces and the triangles cut from the 3 1/2" leaf color in this order:

8. Using a generous 1/4" seam allowance (1/4" plus two threads), sew in the vertical rows, allowing a 1/4" tip to hang over on each of the medium triangles.

9. Sew in the horizontal rows.

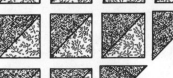

10. Add a medium triangle to one side.

11. Press flat.

12. Straighten the edges. Do not trim off the 1/4" seam allowances.

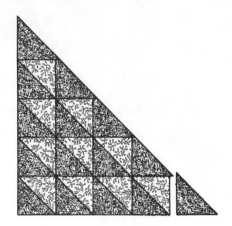

Making the

1. Press under the raw edges 1/4" on the rectangle and triangles cut from the dark stem color.

2. Press in a center fold on the light background triangle.

3. Position the stem on the background triangle, overlapping the rectangle on the small triangles.

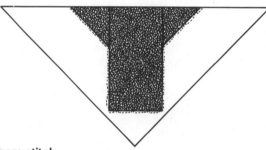

4. Stitch around the stem with invisible thread and a blind hem stitch.

5. Sew the triangle to the Patch Blossoms.

6. Square up to 12 1/2" as closely as you can without trimming off any seam allowances.

Patch blossom is the third block in the fourth horizontal row.

(Optional) Machine Quilted Finish - Refer to page 7.

1. Position Patch Blossoms on the remaining piece of bonded batting.

2. Machine quilt the block.

3. Place side triangles right sides together to Patch Blossoms. Pin.

4. Stitch, and fold back flat.

5. Place the corner triangle right sides together to the block. Pin. Stitch and fold down flat.

6. Sew the sixth diagonal row to the fifth diagonal row, being careful not to catch the batting.

7. Butt the batting together. Hand whip stitch or machine zig zag stitch in place.

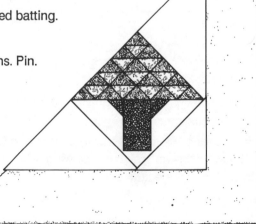

Straightening the Outside Edges of the Blocks

On an unquilted quilt top, you can cut the edges straight. On a machine quilted top, you need to draw on lines and follow those lines when adding the borders.

Unquilted Top

1. Lay an edge of the sewn together quilt top on the cutting board.
2. Place the 1/4" line on the 6" x 24" ruler so that the 1/4" line touches the corner of one quilt block to the other.
3. Trim the side triangle even without removing the seam allowance. Moving the quilt and working from the corners of two blocks at a time, straighten the side triangles.
4. Straighten the corner triangles with the Square Up.

Quilted Top

Lines are measured and drawn on in the above manner once the quilted top is layered with the backing.

Piecing the Quilt Backing

1. Cut the four yards of backing into (2) two yard pieces and remove the selvages.
2. Seam together lengthwise. The seam will appear horizontally across the center back in the finished quilt.

Piecing the Borders

1. Square up the selvage edges.
2. Lay the first border strip right side up. Lay another strip right side to it. Backstitch, stitch the short ends together, and backstitch again.
3. Take the strip on the top and fold it so the right side is up.

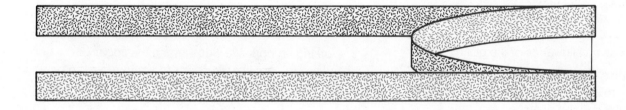

4. Place a third strip right side to it, backstitch, stitch, and backstitch again.
5. Continue flashfeeding all the short ends together into long pieces for each color. Clip the threads.

Binding for the Machine Quilted Quilt (Optional)

Flashfeed the 3" wide binding strips together into one long strip in the same manner.

Finishing the Unquilted Top

The borders may be added to the unquilted top in several different ways. Choose one of these methods, or use your own favorite method.

- Sew the borders to the unquilted top only. Finish with a quick turn.

- Sew the borders through the backing, batting, and unquilted top. Finish the outside edge with a straight piece binding. Follow the instructions for the machine quilted top beginning on page 43.

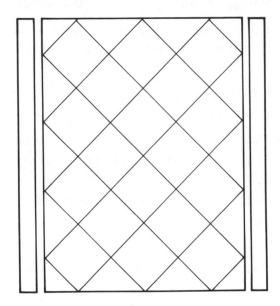

Sewing on the Borders to the Unquilted Top Only

1. Measure the two long sides of the quilt. Cut two equal pieces from the first border color.

2. Place one piece right sides together to one long side, and pin. Stitch.

3. Add the border to the opposite side.

4. Unfold both border pieces back and flat.

5. Measure the two remaining sides from the outside edge of one border to the other. Cut two equal pieces from the first border color.

6. Sew on these two pieces and the pieces from the second border color in the same manner.

Sewing the Unquilted Top to the Backing

1. Place the quilt top right sides together to the backing.

2. Pin around the outside edge.

3. Stitch around the outside edge, leaving a 15" opening in the middle of one side.

Quick Turning the Unquilted Top

1. Lay the bonded batting out flat. Place the quilt on top. Trim away any excess batting. (Optional - Whipstitch the edges of the batting to the seam allowance of the quilt.)

2. Station a person at each corner of the quilt. Begin rolling tightly in each corner and the sides toward the opening.

3. Open up the opening over this wad of fabric and batting, and pop the quilt right side out through the hole.

4. Unroll it right side out carefully with the layers together.

5. Working on opposite sides, grasp the edges of the quilt and pull in opposite directions to smooth out the batting.

6. Whipstitch the opening shut.

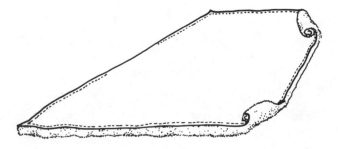

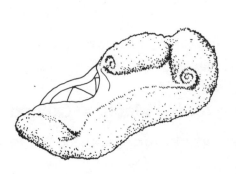

Tying Down Either a Quilted or Unquilted Top

1. Smooth the quilt on a table or large floor area.

2. Thread a curved needle with a long piece of all six strands of embroidery floss or pearl cotton for multiple tying.

3. Working from the center blocks out, take a stitch through all thicknesses in one corner of each block. Without clipping the threads, pull the floss to the next corner, and take a stitch. Stitch all four corners with one continuous strand. Stitch as many points in the patchwork as you choose.

4. Clip the threads.

5. Take the floss on the right and wrap it twice around the floss on the left. Pull both pieces tight.

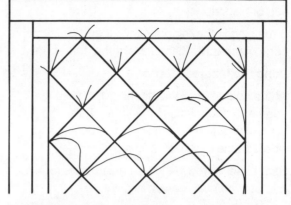

6. Take the floss on the left and wrap it twice around the floss on the right. Pull both pieces tight into a "surgeon's square knot".

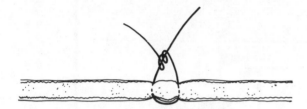

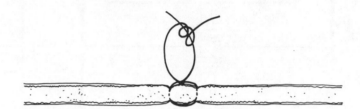

7. Clip the strands even to 1/2" length.

8. Whipstitch the opening shut.

Finishing the Machine Quilted Top

Layering the Quilt and Straightening the Sides

1. Spread out the quilt backing on a large table or floor area with the right side down. Clamp the fabric to the edge of the table with binder clips, or tape the backing to the floor.

2. Center the machine quilted top with batting on the backing. The quilt top is right side up. Smooth until all layers are flat.

3. Safety pin the layers together next to the corners of each block and in the center of each solid square.

4. Draw the 1/4" lines to straighten the side and corner triangles by following the information on page 41.

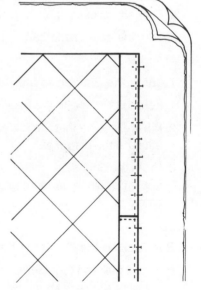

Adding the Borders

1. Place the first border right sides together to a long side, lining up the edge of the border with the 1/4" marked line.

2. Pin together through all layers. Trim away the excess border.

3. Change your stitch length to 10 stitches per inch. Match the bobbin color of thread to the backing.

4. Stitch the border through all thicknesses.

To avoid puckering, always run your right hand along the back, checking before you sew. With your left hand, stretch all layers away from you, and with your right hand, stretch all layers toward you while stitching.

5. Add on the opposite border the length of the quilt. Unfold both long border strips back and flat.

6. Repeat with the top and bottom strips of the first border color.

7. Sew on the second border in the same manner.

Adding the Binding

1. Press the binding strip in half lengthwise with right sides out. Turn under a 1/2" hem and press on the narrow end of the strip.

2. Beginning in the middle of one long side, match the raw edge of the binding strip right sides together to the raw edge of the quilt. Stitch toward the corner.

Making the Mitered Corner

1. At the corner, stop the stitching 1/4" from the edge with the needle in the fabric. Raise the presser foot and turn the quilt to the next side. Put the foot back down.

2. Stitch backwards 1/4", raise the presser foot, and pull the quilt forward slightly.

3. Fold the binding strip straight up on the diagonal. Fingerpress in the diagonal fold.

4. Fold the binding strip straight down with the diagonal fold underneath. Line up the top of the fold with the raw edge of the binding underneath.

5. Begin sewing 1/4" in from the edge at the original pivot point.

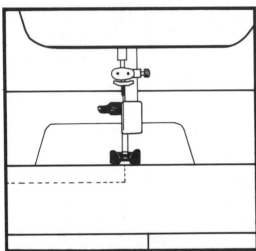
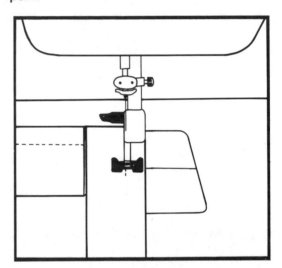

6. Continue stitching and mitering the corners around the outside of the quilt. Avoid seams hitting at corners.

7. End it by overlapping the strip 1/2" at the beginning point.

8. Trim off the excess binding strip.

9. Trim the batting and backing up to the raw edge of the binding.

Turning the Binding to the Back

1. Fold the binding to the back side of the quilt.

2. Pin in place so that the folded edge on the binding covers the stitching line. Tuck in the excess fabric at the miter on the diagonal.

3. From the right side, "stitch in the ditch" around the binding. Use the invisible thread on the right side of the quilt, and a bobbin thread to match the binding on the wrong side of the quilt. Catch the edge of the binding with the stitching.

Bar Tacking the Corners of the Blocks

Hold the quilt top together to the backing with embroidery floss and surgeon's square knots (See previous page) or with bar tacks.

1. Place the invisible thread in the top of the machine and a thread to match the backing in the bobbin.

2. At each corner of each block, place the needle in the depth of the seam, and stitch back and forth 1/4" several times.

3. Clip the threads.

Order Information:

If you do not have a fine quilt shop in your area, you may write for a complete catalog and current price list of all books and patterns published by Quilt in a Day®

Books

Quilt in a Day Log Cabin
The Sampler -- A Machine Sewn Quilt
Trio of Treasured Quilts
Lover's Knot Quilt
Amish Quilt in a Day
Irish Chain in a Day
Country Christmas
Bunnies and Blossoms
May Basket Quilt
Schoolhouse Wallhanging
Diamond Log Cabin Tablecloth or Treeskirt
Morning Star Quilt
Trip Around the World Quilt
Friendship Quilt
Creating With Color
Dresden Plate Quilt, a Simplified Method
Pineapple Quilt, a Piece of Cake
Radiant Star Quilt
Blazing Star Tablecloth

Booklets and Patterns

Patchwork Santa
Last Minute Gifts
Miniature May Basket
Dresden Plate Placemats and Tea Cozy
Angel of Antiquity
Log Cabin Wreath
Log Cabin Christmas Tree
Flying Geese Quilt
Miniature May Basket Wallhanging
Tulip Table Runner and Wall Hanging
Heart's Delight, Nine-Patch Variations

Supplies Available

Rotary Cutters
Rotary Replacement Blades
Cutting Mats with Grids
6" x 6" Mini Rulers
6" x 12" Rulers
6" x 24" Rulers
12 1/2" x 12 1/2" Square Up Rulers
Cutter Kits
Magnetic Pin Cushions
Invisible Threads
Bicycle Clips
Magnetic Seam Guides
Quilting Pins
Curved Needles
Pin Basting Kits
Fairfield Batting
T-Shirts

Videos for Rent or Purchase

Log Cabin
Ohio Star
Lover's Knot
Irish Chain
Schoolhouse Wallhanging
Diamond Log Cabin
Morning Star Quilt
Trip Around the World
Flying Geese
Block Party Series One Videos
Block Party Series Two Videos
and more!

If you are ever in Southern California, San Diego County, drop by and visit the Quilt in a Day Center. Our quilt shop and classroom is located in the La Costa Meadows Business Park. Write ahead for a current class schedule and map.

Quilt in a Day®
1955 Diamond Street, San Marcos, California 92069
Order Line: 1-800- U2 KWILT(1-800-825-9458)   Information Line: 1-619-591-0081